Hannah Solomon
Photographs by Edward Stevenson

J. B. Lippincott Company/Philadelphia and New York

U.S. Library of Congress Cataloging in Publication Data

Solomon, Hannah.
    Bake bread!

    Bibliography: p.
    SUMMARY: A guide to baking bread which provides a basic recipe plus ways
to vary it, step-by-step photographs demonstrating mixing and kneading techniques, and a chapter on the chemistry of bread.
    1. Bread—Juvenile literature. [1. Bread] I. Stevenson, Edward. II. Title.
TX769.S773   641.8'15   76-18807
ISBN-0-397-31670-4   ISBN-0-397-31671-2 (pbk.)

For Wilma, Lou, and Janet
and in memory of Phil

Contents

How can a nation be great
if its bread tastes like Kleenex?

Julia Child

Why Bake Your Own?

WE EAT A LOT OF BREAD: toast at breakfast, sandwich for lunch, bread or rolls with dinner. And pizza at snack time, or a handful of breadsticks—they're bread, too. In fact, bread is such an important part of our diet that when we say "bread," we often mean food in general. "Our daily bread" is everything we eat. "Bread" has become a shorthand way of referring to all the necessities of life. A breadwinner is a person who supports a family, and the job that enables a breadwinner to do so is called that person's bread and butter.

Most of the bread we eat is baked at enormous commercial bakeries and sold in packages at supermarkets. When we buy commercial bread, it may be several days old. It may contain—in addition to the flour, sugar, and other things that belong in bread—azodicarbonamide, calcium stearoyl-2-lactylate, succinylated monoglycerides, and other ingredients that twist our tongues even to pronounce. Commercial bread isn't cheap to buy. And saddest of all, most of it has very little taste and almost no smell. Think back to the last slice of packaged bread you ate—can you remember what it smelled like?

If you bake bread yourself, you know what's in it. Bread can be good—even memorable—food, if you use good nourishing ingredients. Homemade bread is delicious: fresh out of the

9

oven or later on, toasted or plain. The steps that produce a loaf of bread are easy to do, and it's exciting to watch the combined ingredients take on a life of their own and go to work for you. The smell of bread baking is indescribably wonderful, and you can count on everyone who gets a whiff to be on the spot when your finished loaf comes out of the oven. Most satisfying of all is to know that the perfect brown crusty loaf is something *you* made. (If you can bear to part with it, a loaf of home-baked bread is always a warmly received gift.)

As you become an experienced baker, you can produce bread that's just the way you like it—crisp or soft crust, round or square or braided loaf, oatmeal or cornmeal. You'll discover (if you have any left over long enough to find out) that although your bread contains no chemical preservatives, it will stay fresh longer than commercial bread. Bread kept soft and moist by the addition of chemicals is a perfect breeding ground for mold. Your bread will still be wholesome—terrific for toasting—when commercial bread has grown a long gray beard. An additional bonus is that the bread you bake yourself costs considerably less than store bread.

This book will take you step by step through the making of Basic Bread. Our Basic Bread is a plain white loaf, delicious on its own, perfect for slicing to make sandwiches and toast. The other breads in this book use extra ingredients with the basic recipe to produce a whole range of flavors in a variety of shapes.

Before you begin, make sure you have the equipment and ingredients you will need (pages 11–13), and read through the Basic Bread recipe. Once you've learned the ways of Basic Bread, you will be able to approach any bread recipe with confidence.

What You Will Need

EQUIPMENT

A measuring cup, a set of measuring spoons, and *a small bowl or cup* for measuring and preparing ingredients.

A large bowl for mixing and rising the dough. It should hold 2½ to 3 quarts. To check, fill your bowl with measuring cupfuls of water; it should hold 10 to 12. Your bowl should be at least 4½ inches high, so the dough can rise upward instead of just spreading out.

A wooden spoon for mixing (optional). Mixing the ingredients together is much easier to do with your hands, but you can use a spoon if you prefer.

Plastic wrap (recommended) or *a clean dish towel.*

A loaf pan 8½ inches long, 4½ inches wide, and 2½ inches high, or any ovenproof container at least that high holding 5 to 7 cups. Bread can be baked in a container of any shape, but for a good tall loaf the sides should not be lower than 2½ inches.

A clean spray mist bottle (recommended) or *a basting brush* or *pastry brush* (optional).

A single-edge razor blade (recommended) or *a sharp knife.*

A wire rack (recommended, but optional).

An oven. If you're not sure that the oven you're using has a reliable thermostat, it's a good idea to check the temperature with an oven thermometer before putting in the bread.

INGREDIENTS

Yeast. Yeast is a kind of plant. It makes bubbles in bread dough that expand, causing the dough to rise.

  Active dry yeast is the easiest kind to keep and to use. It is a grayish powder that comes in ¼-ounce foil packets, sold in groups of three. Each recipe in this book calls for one packet (¼ ounce) of active dry yeast.

Yeast should be stored, unopened, in the refrigerator or another cool place until you're ready to use it. Try to use it before the date stamped on the package; it's supposedly guaranteed good until that date. (It may be all right afterward, too, but if it doesn't start bubbling in step 1d, don't use it.)

Sugar. Ordinary granulated (white) sugar.

Water. Ordinary drinking water.

Flour. White all-purpose flour made from wheat is the easiest kind to work with and is called for in every recipe in this book. I prefer unbleached flour to bleached flour, which has been treated with chemicals to whiten it, but you can use either kind with good results.

All flour doesn't behave the same way. Some brands absorb more liquid than others. There may even be a difference between two bags of the same brand. Sometimes, depending on your flour (and on other things like the dampness of the weather), you may need to use a little extra flour to keep the dough from being too sticky. You should be prepared for this possibility. The recipes in this book tell you to hold ½ cup of flour in reserve, just in case.

Self-rising flour, cake flour, pastry flour, and "instant blending" flour are designed for other uses. Do not use them to make the breads in this book. They will not work.

Salt. Ordinary table salt.

Oil. Best is a good-quality vegetable oil with little or no flavor of its own. Safflower oil and peanut oil are especially good, but any salad oil or cooking oil can be used. Don't use olive oil, unless you want your bread to taste like olive oil (an exception is pizza, which many people prefer made with olive oil). You can, if you wish, use melted butter or margarine instead, but this means getting another pan dirty.

TIME AND SPACE

Time. Making bread takes time. It doesn't require your attention every minute; you're on your own while the dough is rising and while it's baking, which is most of the time involved. But you must be available over a period of three to four hours, to take care of the various steps as the moment for each arrives. When you bake bread—especially the first few times you try it—be sure you have a good long stretch of uninterrupted free time. You can slow down the rising process by refrigerating the dough (page 40) or delay the baking by letting the dough rise one more time. But until you've baked bread at least once, don't make the process more complicated with deadlines or distractions.

And—no matter how experienced a baker you become—you *can't* decide at five o'clock to bake bread for dinner at six. Impossible.

Space. You'll need a place to work: to assemble your ingredients, mix them together, and knead the dough. For kneading, you'll want a table or countertop with a surface that can be scrubbed. It should be sturdy enough not to tip over or slide around, and low enough so you can rest your palms comfortably on it with your arms slightly bent.

Plan to bake bread at a time when you won't be in anyone else's way—or vice versa. Make sure someone else isn't planning to use the oven—at a different temperature. Because mixing and kneading can be messy, choose a workplace that's

14

easy to clean up. You might cover the floor around your workplace with newspapers to protect it from flying flour. Protect your clothes with an apron.

A CAUTION

Knives, razor blades, and ovens are not dangerous by themselves—only in the hands of someone who is inexperienced or who is not concentrating. When using a sharp blade of any kind, make sure your other hand is not in the path of the blade. Also, make sure you know the proper procedure for lighting the oven. *Give any potentially dangerous procedure your full attention.*

Basic Bread

BASIC BREAD IS A FIRM-TEXTURED and slightly chewy white bread with a crisp crust. The recipe makes one loaf about 8½″ × 4½″ × 4″ which weighs about 1½ pounds. This amount of dough is easy to handle. When you are an experienced baker, you may want to try recipes in other books that make several loaves.

These are the steps in bread making:

1. *Preparing the dough.* The ingredients are mixed together.
2. *Kneading.* The dough is folded, flattened, and turned until it becomes elastic.
3. *Rising.* The dough stands in a warm place until it expands to double its original size.
4. *Shaping the loaf.* The dough is deflated, formed into a loaf, and placed in the prepared pan.
5. *Second rising.* The dough rises again until double in size.
6. *Baking.* The loaf is baked in the oven until done.

These same steps are used in making all the breads in this book.

Before you begin, read through to page 39. Make sure you have the equipment and ingredients you need. Roll up your sleeves, take off rings and bracelets and watches, and wash your hands.

What you will need:

EQUIPMENT

measuring cup
small bowl
measuring spoons
large bowl
plastic wrap
loaf pan
spray mist bottle
single-edge razor blade
wire rack

INGREDIENTS

½ cup of warm water
2 teaspoons of sugar
1 packet (¼ ounce) of active dry yeast
3¼ cups of flour plus ½ cup of flour
2 teaspoons of salt
2 tablespoons of oil, plus enough warm water to
    make ¾ cup
1 teaspoon of oil for the bowl
1 teaspoon of oil for the pan

1. PREPARING THE DOUGH

1a. Measure ½ cup of warm water. It should feel warm, not hot, to your finger. Pour it into the small bowl. Add 2 teaspoons of sugar and 1 packet (¼ ounce) of yeast. Stir with your fingers until you can no longer feel sugar grains at the bottom.

1b. Measure 3¼ cups of flour into the large bowl. To measure flour, spoon it into the measuring cup and level it off with a flat

knife, letting the extra fall back into the flour bag or canister. Measure an extra ½ cup of flour and set it aside.

1c. Add 2 teaspoons of salt to the flour in the bowl.

1d. Pour 2 tablespoons of oil into the measuring cup. Add enough warm water to fill the cup to the ¾-cup mark. Pour the oil and water mixture into the large bowl.

1e. Blend the oil and water mixture with the flour by squeezing it through your fingers. If you mix with one hand, you can keep the other hand clean for reaching and measuring. Scrape any dough that clings to your fingers back into the bowl.

1f. By now, the yeast mixture in the small bowl should look foamy, with small bubbles at the top. If you don't see bubbles, wait a few minutes; yeast works slowly if the water or the room is cool. When bubbles appear, pour the yeast mixture into the large bowl.

1g. Now mix the dough well with your fingers, turning it over and squeezing it until it is evenly blended. The dough should begin to hold together in a somewhat sticky mass. Use it to clean any dry flour off the sides and bottom of the bowl.

If the dough is very wet and sticky and clings to the bowl and to your hand, add a little flour (start with a big pinch) from the reserved half cup. Add just enough to make the dough hold together.

1h. When the dough is well mixed, take a big pinch of flour from the reserved half cup and spread it over your kneading surface, covering a space about a foot square. Now turn the contents of the bowl out onto the floured surface. Scrape any dough that clings to your fingers and to the bowl off onto the ball. The dough will be limp and ragged-looking. It will feel slightly warm and lumpy, and if you pull a piece off the ball, it will come away easily.

Put the large bowl in the sink and fill it with warm water, so it will soak clean while you knead.

2. KNEADING

2a. Push your thumbs into the middle of the dough.

2b. Fold the dough in half toward you.

2c. Press it firmly down and away from you with the heels of your hands.

2d. Turn the dough around so that the part that was nearest you is now on your right.

Continue to knead by repeating these four steps. You can push and bang the dough around as hard as you want. Kneading doesn't have to be done exactly like this, though many people find this way easiest; as long as you keep folding, flattening, and turning the dough, you can do it however you like.

If the dough sticks to the board or to your hands, rub board or hands with a little of the reserved flour. If you add too much flour the bread will be tough and dry, so add only as much as you need to keep the dough from being too sticky to work with.

As you knead the dough, its texture will change. It will become smooth and the outside of the ball will develop a satiny feel. The dough will also become elastic; folding it over will become more difficult, and the dough will stubbornly spring back into a ball. If you pull a piece of the dough with your fingers, it will stretch instead of breaking off as in step 1h. If you get tired of kneading, stop and rest a minute, or get a friend to knead for a while.

Finally, shallow, wrinkly cracks will appear on the surface of the dough. This is a sign that you have kneaded it enough.

You can stop kneading; or, if you are enjoying it, knead for a little while longer—it won't hurt the bread. Depending on how fast you work and how vigorously you handle the dough, kneading will probably take 3 to 10 minutes.

Shape the kneaded dough into a neat ball and let it rest on the kneading surface.

2e. Wash the large bowl and dry it well. Pour 1 teaspoon of oil into the bowl and rub it all around with your fingers.

2f. Wipe any oil off your fingers onto the ball of dough. Put the dough in the oiled bowl, top side down, then turn it over so that the ball is oiled on all sides.

Cover the bowl with transparent plastic wrap to keep the dough from drying out. You can cover it instead with a clean dish towel which has been soaked in water and wrung out well, but the plastic will let you watch the dough rise without uncovering it. Try to imagine how big a ball made from twice that much dough would be.

3. RISING

3a. Set the bowl in a warm place. If it gets too hot, the yeast will be killed and the dough will not rise. Do not put the bowl over a lighted stove burner, in a hot oven, or directly on a hot radiator, for example. Good places for bread to rise include: inside the turned-off oven, with pans of hot water on a lower shelf (or without, if the oven has a pilot light); on a rack above the pilot light of a gas stove; on a pillow on top of a radiator; on a sunny windowsill; on a refrigerator or other applicance that is warm on top. Or you can set the bowl in the sink, in a large pan or on a rack over a large pan, and run warm water into the sink or pan. If you do this, add hot water as the water cools off, and try not to get water on the dough. Or you can find your own place.

Feel the bottom and sides of the bowl and look at the dough every 15 or 20 minutes, especially the first time you leave dough to rise in a particular place. If the bowl is warmer on one side than the other, turn it around. If it feels hot, move it away from the heat.

Once the dough starts to rise, the ball will be slightly larger each time you look. It will probably be flatter, too. If the dough is not rising, or if the bowl feels cold, move it to a warmer place—or be prepared to wait a long time. Dough will rise at cool temperatures—even in the refrigerator—but much, much more slowly.

3b. Rising will probably take between 45 and 90 minutes, depending on the temperature of the room and of the water you used. Dough that has risen enough will have almost doubled; it will be nearly twice the size it was in step 2f. It will no longer be as elastic as it was in step 2d. If the ball looks big

28

enough, test its elasticity by poking your finger about ½ inch into it. If the hole closes up, cover the bowl, wait 15 or 20 minutes, and test again. The hole should just stay there when you pull out your finger. It's important to let the dough rise enough; otherwise, the bread will probably be dense and soggy.

4. SHAPING THE LOAF

4a. When the dough has risen enough, interrupt the rising process by punching it down. Push your fist into the middle of the dough. Air will escape in a rush, and the dough will collapse. Fold the edges of the ball in toward the middle, pushing firmly to press out air bubbles.

Take the dough out of the bowl and set it on the kneading surface. Knead it firmly a few times. Form it into a ball. Set the ball aside for about 10 minutes. Letting the dough "rest" makes it less elastic and easier to handle.

4b. To prepare the baking pan, pour 1 teaspoon of oil into the pan. Spread the oil all around the inside of the pan with your fingers, making sure the corners and sides are coated with oil.

4c. To make a loaf free of air pockets and streaks, start by pressing the dough flat with your fingers. Push it out into a rectangle about 1 inch thick and a little wider than the pan is long; measure it against the pan as you work. If the dough is too elastic and springs back instead of lying flat, let it rest for 3 or 4 minutes before trying again.

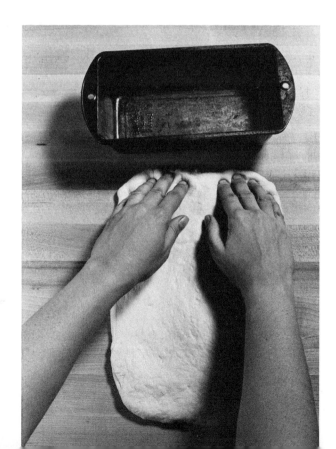

4d. When the dough is flattened, begin rolling it firmly into a cylinder. As you roll, press with your fingers to join the dough onto the cylinder.

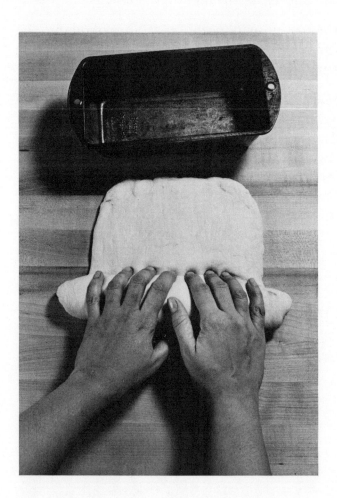

4e. When the dough is rolled, pinch the seam closed.

4f. Turning the ends under slightly, place the loaf in the oiled

pan, seam side down. Press it gently to even it out. Make sure the dough is touching all four sides of the pan.

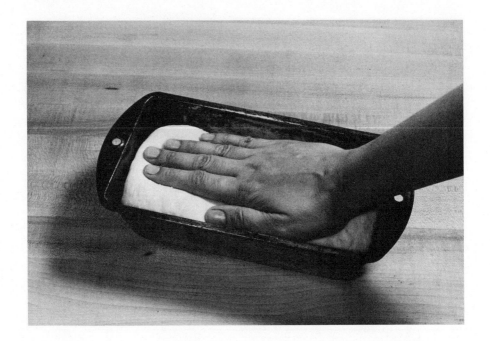

5. SECOND RISING

5a. Cover the pan with plastic wrap. Put the pan of dough in a warm place. The second rising will not take as long as the first—maybe only half as long. When it has risen enough, it will be almost twice the size it was in step 4f. In an 8½" × 4½" × 2½" loaf pan, the center of the dough will have risen slightly above the top of the pan. Don't use the poke test—you don't want finger holes in your finished loaf—but you can press gently, if you like, to make sure the dough isn't elastic.

While the dough is rising, you can clean up your workplace. Brush any dry flour off the kneading surface and scrub surface with a plastic or nylon scouring pad (a metal one may scratch). Wash floury utensils in hot water; cold water will turn the flour to paste.

When the dough has risen as high as the top of the pan, turn on the oven and heat it to 400 degrees.

5b. Remove the plastic wrap. To prepare the loaf for baking, spray or brush the top *lightly* with water. This will make the crust extra crisp. A spray mist bottle is the easiest way to do this lightly and evenly, but you can use a brush, a moistened paper towel, or your fingers.

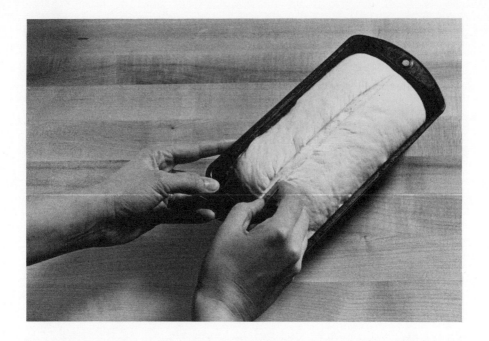

5c. With a single-edge razor blade or sharp knife, carefully cut a slash about ½ inch deep right down the center of the loaf. The bread will rise so fast in the oven that the crust can't expand fast enough, and if you do not slash the loaf it will crack open—probably along one side—as it bakes. The slashed top will spread open as the bread rises and give the loaf a very professional appearance. (The loaf may crack anyway, but this won't hurt the bread.) Several diagonal slashes also make a handsome loaf (see page 46).

6. BAKING

6a. Put the bread in the preheated oven. Center the pan on a shelf about halfway up, so that heat can circulate on all sides. Once the loaf is in the oven, do not open the door for 35 minutes.

6b. After 35 minutes, the loaf should be fully risen—an inch or two above the top of the pan—and beautifully brown. Protecting your hands with potholders, take it out of the oven.

Turn the pan over so that the loaf slides out onto a countertop or other heatproof surface. If the bread sticks to the pan, run a knife blade carefully around the edge of the loaf to loosen it. Try not to puncture the crust.

Tap the bottom of the loaf gently with your knuckles or fingertips. If it sounds hollow—almost as though you were tapping a wooden tabletop or an empty box—it is done. If you hear a dull rubbery thud, the bread is not done. Put the loaf back in the oven—without the pan—for 5 minutes before testing it again. (Baking it briefly without the pan will make the side and bottom crust crisper.) If necessary, bake it 5 or 10 minutes more.

It's not easy to recognize the sound of a finished loaf from the description in a book, but with practice you will be able to tell accurately every time. Underdone bread is wet and doughy, and once you've sliced it there's no going back. But if your oven is accurate, the bread will almost certainly be done after 50 minutes of baking.

When the bread is done, take it out, and turn off the oven.

6c. When the bread is finished and removed from its pan, put it on a wire rack to cool. This is important; if air does not circulate freely around the hot loaf, the crust will get steamy and soggy. If you don't have a rack, set the loaf crosswise on top of the loaf pan, or invent another way to let the air get to all sides of the loaf.

There's your bread! It's almost impossible to resist cutting a slice as soon as it's out of the oven, but if you can bear to wait, it will slice more easily and the texture will be better after it has cooled to lukewarm. Be sure you let it cool completely before putting it in a plastic bag or other container. See page 69 for suggestions on slicing and storing bread.

The next time you bake bread, the directions will be much easier to follow. Make Basic Bread again, to make sure you've got all the techniques under control—or try baking one of the different kinds of bread described in the following pages.

What If . . . ?

If you live at a very high altitude, your bread will rise especially fast. Watch it carefully.

If you want to bake bread in a glass pan, set your oven at 375 degrees instead of 400.

If the yeast mixture does not bubble, it can mean one of three things:

1. Water too cool to start the yeast working; put the bowl containing the mixture in a warm place, and wait 10 minutes.

2. Water too hot, so it killed the yeast. If you used hot water instead of warm, start over.

3. A defective packet of yeast. This happens very rarely, but it's possible. Try another packet—and if you're sure that's the problem (and the date stamped on the packet hasn't passed), notify the manufacturer.

If the bread doesn't rise, it almost certainly means that it's not warm enough (assuming you've "proved" your yeast by making it bubble). Move the bowl to a warmer spot. (If the bowl is in a really hot place, you may have killed the yeast by overheating it.)

If you have to stop work in the middle, you can punch the dough down at any point and put it in the refrigerator in its bowl or in a plastic bag. It will go on rising, but much more slowly. It won't hurt the dough to have an extra rising, or even two; punch it down if it seems to be getting near double in size. When you're ready, take the dough out, put it in a warm place, and let it finish rising—then go on with the recipe.

If you don't punch the dough down when it has doubled, it will go on rising—and eventually collapse. It will rise again, so you can make bread from it, but the finished loaf will be coarse and chewy, with a strong yeast flavor. Some people like it that way.

If the finished loaf has big holes in it, it probably means one of two things:

   1. Big air bubbles were left in the dough after the first

rising. Be sure to get bubbles out when punching the dough down and shaping the loaf.

2. You rolled the dough too loosely when shaping the loaf, so air spaces were left. Be sure to make a tight roll.

If the finished loaf has a heavy dense streak at the bottom, you probably didn't let the dough rise enough the second time.

If the finished loaf is wet and doughy in the middle, you probably didn't bake it long enough. Bake it longer next time and listen carefully to the sound it makes when you thump it.

If you want a glazed crust and you haven't made egg bread, a small amount of egg, egg yolk, or egg white mixed with an equal amount of water or milk can be used. It seems wasteful to crack an egg in order to use just a little bit of it; but you might have another use for the rest.

Some Different Breads

YOU CAN VARY BASIC BREAD by adding or substituting a new ingredient. Each of these variants has a surprisingly different quality. Bread dough that contains other types of flour tends to feel stickier and less elastic than dough made entirely from white flour.

WHOLE WHEAT BREAD

This whole wheat bread is light in texture and light tan in color. Because it calls for a rather small amount of whole wheat flour, it is not as dense and chewy as some whole wheat breads.

Whole wheat flour can be bought at some supermarkets and at health food stores. It should be stored in the refrigerator or

a cool place; since it contains more of the oily part of the wheat than white flour does, it can spoil if kept too warm or for too long.

To make whole wheat bread, follow the directions for Basic Bread, but in step 1b, put ½ cup of whole wheat flour and 2¾ cups of white flour (instead of 3¼ cups of white flour) into the large bowl.

Whole wheat bread dough will feel slightly granular.

OATMEAL BREAD

Oatmeal bread has a slightly rougher texture than Basic Bread and is light beige in color instead of creamy white. It has a nice grainy taste.

To make oatmeal bread, follow the directions for Basic Bread, but in step 1b, add ¾ cup of dry uncooked oatmeal (rolled oats) to the bowl with the 3¼ cups of flour.

Oatmeal bread dough will feel coarser than Basic Bread dough.

CORNMEAL BREAD

Cornmeal bread is pale yellow in color. It has a pleasant cornmeal taste and the crunchy, slightly gritty texture of good cornbread. It makes especially good toast.

To make cornmeal bread, follow the directions for Basic

Bread, but in step 1b add ½ cup of dry uncooked yellow cornmeal to the bowl with the 3¼ cups of flour.

Cornmeal bread dough will have a somewhat gritty feel.

WHEAT GERM BREAD

Wheat germ gives this bread a speckled appearance, a nutty texture, a rich wheat flavor, and a generous helping of protein, vitamins, and iron. You can buy wheat germ in a health food store or in the cereal section of many supermarkets. Like whole wheat flour, wheat germ should be kept in a cool place.

To make wheat germ bread, follow the directions for Basic

Bread, but in step 1b add ½ cup of plain (unsweetened) wheat germ to the bowl along with the 3¼ cups of flour.

CHEESE BREAD

This bread is lightly flavored with cheese and makes delicious sandwiches. You can use sharp cheddar cheese, a hard Italian cheese like Parmesan, or a mixture of both.

To make cheese bread, follow the directions for Basic Bread, but in step 1b add ½ cup of grated cheese to the 3¼ cups of flour in the bowl. Use more cheese—up to 2 cups—if you want a more pronounced cheese flavor.

47

EGG BREAD WITH GLAZED CRUST

Adding an egg makes a rich bread with a characteristic tender texture. Part of the egg is saved and brushed on top of the loaf to give the crust a shiny glaze.

To make egg bread, follow the directions for Basic Bread, steps 1a–1c.

1d. Break 1 large egg into your measuring cup and then fill the cup to the ¾-cup mark with warm water. Mix the egg and water together with a fork. With measuring spoon, put 2 tablespoons of the egg and water mixture into a small bowl or cup. Set it aside.

Now add 2 tablespoons of oil to what remains in the

measuring cup, and add this mixture to the flour mixture in the large bowl.

Continue with directions for Basic Bread, steps 1e–5a.

5b. Instead of brushing or spraying the top of the loaf with water, stir the reserved egg and water mixture and then brush a thin coat of it over the top of the loaf. If you wish, you can sprinkle the loaf with poppy seeds or sesame seeds; they will stick to the glaze.

Continue with the directions for Basic Bread, steps 5c–6c.

Some Different Shapes

INSTEAD OF BAKING YOUR BREAD in a loaf pan, try a round or braided loaf—or breadsticks.

ROUND LOAF

Any of these breads can be baked on a cookie sheet as a round loaf. A sprinkling of cornmeal keeps the loaf from sticking to the cookie sheet and makes the bottom crust extra crunchy.

To make a round loaf, follow any of the bread recipes, steps 1a–4a.

4b. Sprinkle a cookie sheet with 2 teaspoons of cornmeal. Set the ball of dough on it.

Skip steps 4c–4f, since the round loaf is already formed.

5a. Cover the dough loosely with plastic wrap and let it rise (see Basic Bread, step 5a). The ball will flatten and spread somewhat as it rises.

Follow the directions for Basic Bread, step 5b.

5c. Make two or three slashes across the top of the ball of dough, or make two slashes in an X.

Continue with the directions for Basic Bread, step 6.

BRAIDED LOAF

Any of these breads can be baked as a braided loaf, a truly impressive sight. Loaves of egg bread are traditionally formed this way.

51

To make a braided loaf, follow any of the bread recipes, steps 1a–4a. Before letting the dough rest in step 4a, cut it into three equal pieces with a sharp knife.

4b. Grease a cookie sheet with 1 teaspoon of oil.

4c. Pull and roll each of the three pieces of dough into a rope, about 13 inches long and 1¼ inches thick in the middle. It can be thinner at the ends. Handle the dough firmly, but avoid tearing it. If the dough is too elastic and springs back instead of stretching, let the piece you're working on rest for 3 or 4 minutes before trying it again.

4d. Put one of the dough ropes on the greased cookie sheet, at a slant so that it points toward your right hand (1). Put another strip across it, forming an X (2). Lay the third strip on top, straight up and down (3).

4e. To braid, start in the middle. Cross strip 1 over strip 3, then strip 2 over strip 1. Continue crossing first the right-hand strip, then the left-hand strip, over the middle strip.

4f. When you reach the end, pinch the ends of the strips together and turn them under. Turn the cookie sheet around so the unbraided end is facing you. Braid the strips on this side, starting with the right-hand one. Pinch the ends together and turn them under.

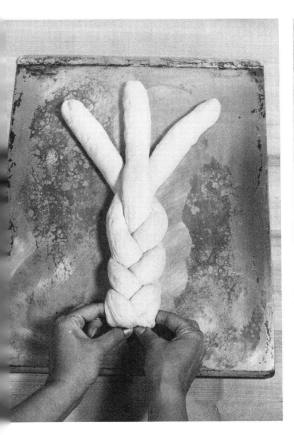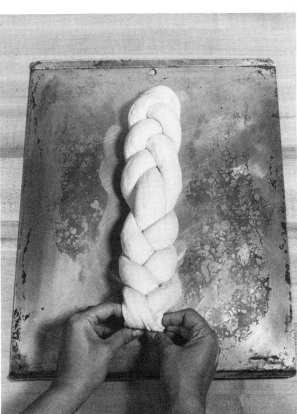

4g. Drape a piece of plastic wrap loosely over the loaf.

Continue with the directions for Basic Bread, step 5. The loaf will flatten out somewhat during the second rising. In step 5b, if you are making braided egg bread, brush the top and sides of the loaf with the glaze before baking, and sprinkle it with poppy seeds or sesame seeds if you wish. Do not slash a braided loaf.

Follow the remaining directions for Basic Bread, step 6.

BREADSTICKS

Any of these bread doughs can be baked into crunchy bread-sticks. They may not be as thin and even as the kind you buy, but they will have a wonderful fresh bread taste. One recipe for bread dough will make about 48 breadsticks about 7 inches long. You can make bread dough and use part of it for breadsticks and part for pizza.

Note that breadsticks are baked at 350 degrees, instead of 400; slow baking makes them crisp and dry all the way through.

To make breadsticks, you will need a batch of any bread dough, plus about 2 tablespoons of cornmeal. For shaping and baking, you will need a rolling pin, a sharp knife, and a cookie sheet.

Follow any of the bread recipes, steps 1–4a.

4b. Sprinkle 1 tablespoon of cornmeal over the cookie sheet.

4c. Roll the dough out about 12 inches square and about ⅜ inch thick. If the dough is too elastic and springs back instead of stretching, wait 3 or 4 minutes before trying again.

4d. Cut the dough in half lengthwise. Now cut each of the two 12-inch strips of dough into slices about ½ inch wide. Each strip should make about 24 slices. It's important to make the sticks thin, so they will be crisp all the way through.

5a. Lay the sticks on the cookie sheet about 1 inch apart. When all the sticks are shaped, turn the oven on to 350 degrees. Let the sticks rise while the oven is heating (10 to 15 minutes).

5b. Spray or brush the sticks with water. If you have used egg bread dough, brush the sticks with glaze, and if you like, sprinkle each with a pinch of poppy seeds or sesame seeds.

6a. Center the cookie sheet in the preheated oven and bake the sticks for 30 minutes or until they are deep golden brown. To test for doneness, take one out and cut or break it in half. It should be hard all the way through, with no soft center. Let the sticks cool on a wire rack.

Two Special Breads

HERE ARE TWO RECIPES that show some of the fancier things that can be done with bread dough. They involve a few more ingredients and a few more steps, so try them when you have plenty of time and are feeling confident.

PIZZA

Pizza crust is really just bread, and Basic Bread makes a thin crisp pizza crust. You can substitute olive oil for the oil in the recipe, which will give a nice flavor. One batch of Basic Bread dough will make two 12-inch pizzas or four small (8½-inch) pizzas.

To make two pizzas, you will need one batch of Basic Bread dough, plus about 4 teaspoons of olive or other oil for greasing the cookie sheet or pizza pan. To make topping for two pizzas, you will also need the following:

6 more teaspoons of olive oil

1 8-ounce can of tomato sauce

about 8 ounces of mozzarella cheese (pizza cheese)

½ teaspoon of oregano

pinch of garlic powder, pinch of dried red pepper flakes (optional)

extra topping ingredients (optional): slices of pepperoni or cooked Italian sausage, strips of cooked green pepper, cooked sliced mushrooms, sliced onion, anchovy fillets, etc.

A spoon is helpful for spreading the tomato sauce. For shaping and baking, you will need a rolling pin, and one or two cookie sheets instead of a loaf pan.

To make pizza, follow the directions for Basic Bread, steps 1–4a. In step 1d, you may use olive oil instead of other oil. Before letting the dough rest in step 4a, cut it into two equal parts with a knife.

4b. Pour 2 teaspoons of oil on a cookie sheet and spread it around with your fingers.

4c. Flatten one piece of the dough on the kneading surface. Now, roll it out into a circle about 12 inches in diameter. Use a rolling pin to roll the dough with firm strokes, from the center outward. Pick up the dough and turn it over after every one or two strokes, to make sure all parts are being rolled evenly. If the dough sticks, rub a small amount of flour onto the kneading surface. If it is too elastic and springs back instead of

61

stretching, let it rest for 3 or 4 minutes before trying again. Roll dough until it is about ¼ inch thick; it can be a little thicker at the edges.

4d. When the dough is rolled thin enough, put it on the oiled cookie sheet.

5a. When all your crusts have been rolled, turn on the oven to heat to 450 degrees. Let the crusts rise, uncovered, while the oven is heating (about 15 minutes). Meanwhile, collect the topping ingredients. Cut the mozzarella cheese into small slices or into cubes about ½ inch across.

5b. Drizzle about 1 teaspoon of oil over one pizza crust and spread it around gently with your fingers.

Put ½ cup (half the can) of tomato sauce over the oil on the crust, and spread it around evenly with the back of a spoon, leaving a ½-inch edge uncovered all the way around.

Sprinkle a pinch of oregano (about ¼ teaspoon) over the tomato sauce. If you're using optional topping ingredients, put them on now. If you're using garlic powder and/or red pepper flakes, sprinkle a small pinch over the pizza.

Distribute about 4 ounces of cheese (¾ to 1 cup) evenly over the pizza. Drizzle about 2 teaspoons of oil over all.

6. Place the cookie sheet on the next to bottom shelf of the preheated oven and bake the pizza for about 12 minutes. When done, the edge should be brown and crisp and the cheese should be bubbly. Slice the pizza with a sharp knife or pizza cutter and eat it right away.

You can bake both the pizzas at once, or you can bake one, put the topping on the second while the first is baking, and bake the second while the first is being eaten.

CINNAMON RAISIN SPIRAL BREAD

This may be the most complicated recipe in this book. It takes a certain amount of patience and persistence to flatten a whole batch of bread dough into a thin sheet and roll it up to enclose its cinnamon-sugar filling. But any raisin bread fan will feel the results are worth it. Try it with peanut butter, cream cheese, and/or jam. Try it toasted. Some people think it's good for dessert.

To make cinnamon raisin spiral bread, you will need the ingredients for any bread except cheese bread, plus:

> ½ cup of raisins
> 2 tablespoons of firmly packed brown sugar
> 2 tablespoons of white sugar
> ½ teaspoon of cinnamon

For shaping, you will need a rolling pin.

Follow the directions for any bread, step 1a. In step 1b, add ½ cup of raisins to the flour in the mixing bowl.

Continue with the directions, steps 1c–4b. As you knead this dough, the raisins will tend to pop out on the surface. If any fall off, just push them back into the dough.

4c. Press the dough flat on the kneading surface, using stiff fingers and palms to push out any air bubbles. Rub rolling pin lightly with flour and begin rolling the dough. Roll from the center to the edge farthest from you. After one or two strokes,

pick up the dough and turn it over end to end, and then roll the other way so that the dough is stretched into a long rectangle. The rectangle should be a little wider than the length of your bread pan; measure it against the pan as you work. Keep rolling the dough until it is about ¼ inch thick. If the dough is too elastic and springs back instead of stretching, let it rest for 3 or 4 minutes before trying again. You may have to stop rolling several times to let the dough relax. The finished rectangle should be about 9 inches by 16 inches and ¼ inch thick.

4d. Mix together in a small bowl 2 tablespoons firmly packed brown sugar, 2 tablespoons of white sugar, and ½ teaspoon of cinnamon. Sprinkle this mixture evenly over the rectangle of dough, leaving a ½-inch edge all around.

4e. Now, starting at the side closest to you, roll the dough firmly into a tight cylinder. Roll slowly and evenly, pressing down with stiff fingers to make sure there are no air pockets or bubbles.

When the whole rectangle has been rolled up, wet your fingers and pinch the seams closed, both at the ends and along the side. This is important for keeping the cinnamon and sugar inside the loaf.

Continue with the directions for Basic Bread, steps 4f–6c. It is risky to slash a spiral loaf, since you might cut through to the cinnamon-sugar filling. But if you really want to try it, hold the razor blade almost flat instead of straight up and down, and cut a shallow slice into the loaf sideways.

Even if you are careful, a seam or slash may let the filling through, or the loaf may crack in baking and let it escape. When this happens, dark sugary syrup will bake onto the outside of the loaf and probably onto the pan. This doesn't look elegant, but it will taste just as good as a perfect loaf. If you do have a leaky loaf, put it back into the oven *leaky side up* to brown the bottom crust (step 6b). Soak the pan in hot water to loosen the baked-on syrup.

Slicing, Storing, and Leftovers

USE A SHARP KNIFE FOR SLICING BREAD. Most bread knives have serrated (sawtooth) blades that can cut through the bread without squashing it. When bread is very fresh, the inside is soft and the outside is hard and crisp, so it's difficult to slice it neatly. As bread cools, it gets firmer. After a day or so it can be sliced easily. Try turning the loaf on its side; bread is often easier to slice when you're not trying to cut straight down

through the top crust. If the slices get uneven, turn the loaf over and cut from the other side.

To slice a round loaf, you can start at one end and make slices the usual way. Or you can make wedges as though cutting a cake (this kind of slice isn't good for sandwiches or for toasting). Or you can cut the loaf in half, turn one half cut side down, and make small up-and-down slices.

In any case, don't slice it until you're ready to eat it. Sliced bread dries out much faster than unsliced bread. But there is one exception to this rule: if you plan to store the bread in the freezer, you can slice the whole loaf, freeze it, and then take out and thaw only as many slices as you need.

Bread will stay soft longest if kept in a tightly closed plastic bag, at room temperature or in the refrigerator. Be sure bread has cooled completely before you put it away; otherwise, moisture will collect in the bag and the bread will get moldy. When bread is stored airtight, the crust gradually absorbs moisture from the inside of the loaf and becomes softer as the inside dries out and becomes harder and firmer. If bread is stored where some air can circulate—in a brown paper bag or in an old-fashioned breadbox with airholes—the crust will not soften as much, but the whole loaf will dry out faster.

Bread is at its best within a few hours of baking, but it can go on being good food as long as it lasts. When it gets firmer than you like, try it toasted or as French toast. Or slice it as thinly as possible, spread the slices out on a cookie sheet, and bake it at 250 degrees until it is golden brown—and you have melba

toast to serve with cheese or dips. The length of time it will take depends on how dry it is; start checking after 15 minutes. It's often easier to make really thin slices if you cut the loaf in half first.

Or cut leftover bread into cubes about ¾ inch on each side, bake the cubes the same way, and you have croutons, which you can use to add crunch to soups or salad. Store melba toast and croutons in airtight jars or in the freezer.

Leftover bread that is too hard to slice can be made into bread crumbs. Crumble it by hand, or crush it with a rolling pin, or whirl small chunks in a blender. Store crumbs in a jar or in the freezer for use in meat loaf, casserole toppings, or any recipe that calls for bread crumbs.

How It Works

YOU KNOW WHAT THE INGREDIENTS OF BREAD ARE, and what you do to turn them into bread. But how does this process work? You can bake wonderful bread without knowing what is going on inside the dough; but for the scientifically inclined, here is a brief account of what is taking place (a detailed description could fill a volume).

A loaf of bread is the end product of a series of chemical and physical changes that result from combining three ingredients, allowing them to act on one another over a period of time, and then subjecting them to high heat. These three key ingredients are flour, yeast, and water.

Flour is finely ground grain. Wheat flour is especially suitable for baking bread because wheat contains a high proportion of gluten, a mixture of complex proteins that form a weblike elastic structure in bread dough. A wheat grain or "berry" is made up of several layers. Milling—the process of making wheat into flour—involves several stages of crushing the grain between huge rollers and sifting out the coarse particles of bran (outside layer) and germ (innermost core), leaving the fine particles of endosperm, the portion highest in gluten content. White flour is what remains after about 25 percent of the wheat berry has been discarded, while what we know as whole wheat flour uses from 80 to nearly 100 percent

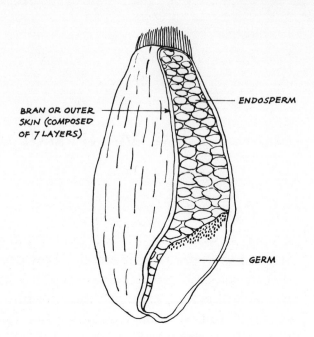

BRAN OR OUTER SKIN (COMPOSED OF 7 LAYERS)

ENDOSPERM

GERM

LENGTHWISE SECTION
OF WHEAT GRAIN

of the berry, including bran and germ. Since the whole wheat flour contains a lower proportion of endosperm than white flour, it also contains a lower proportion of gluten, which makes whole wheat bread dough less elastic and more difficult to work with.

Flour that has just been milled is called "green" flour, although it is actually a yellowish color. If allowed to stand for two to three months, it will age naturally, and the yellowish pigment will bleach out as it reacts with oxygen in the air. Bleaching with chlorine dioxide or other chemicals achieves this aging effect in a much shorter time.

The end product of all this processing—average wheat flour—contains 69 to 72 percent carbohydrates (starch and sugar), 11 to 14 percent proteins (those that form gluten, and others as well), 14.5 percent moisture, 2 percent fat, 1.8 percent vitamins and minerals.

Yeast is composed of single-celled plants so tiny that three thousand or so laid end to end would measure about an inch in length. Yeast cells feed on sugar and produce carbon dioxide and alcohol, and they multiply to produce more yeast cells. The conversion of sugar by yeast is called fermentation, and this is the process by which grains and fruits are turned into alcoholic beverages. Although there are many different types of yeasts, the packages of yeast you buy in the supermarket contain only cells from a single variety especially adapted to making bread rise. Dry yeast is in a dormant ("sleeping") stage and becomes active when in contact with water.

Yeast cells are very choosy about the conditions under which they will convert sugar and multiply. The environment must be moist. The temperature must be above about 50 degrees—below which point the yeast is inactive—and below about 130 degrees, at which point the yeast plants die of overheating. Some sugar is required for the yeast to feed on, but too high a concentration of sugar slows it down or stops its activity altogether. A high concentration of any of a number of substances—among them salt, alcohol, and carbon dioxide—has the same effect.

The water that goes into bread turns the dry flour and yeast into a dough that can be worked. It activates the yeast, providing the moist conditions that the yeast requires. It also changes the gluten-forming proteins of the flour into gluten.

The other ingredients of Basic Bread—oil, salt, and the sugar added at the beginning—are not actually necessary to the baking of bread. The chemical process can go on perfectly well without them. They are added to improve the flavor of the bread and to help it to brown. The oil also helps prevent tearing of the gluten during mixing and helps keep the bread from drying out. The salt keeps the yeast activity somewhat slowed down, giving the bread a uniform, even texture. The added sugar provides a concentrated temporary food source for the yeast, giving fermentation a head start. Although sugar is necessary for fermentation, bread can be made without the addition of sugar because the yeast can feed on the sugar that is present as a component of the flour. Enzymes in the yeast turn part of the flour's starch into sugar as well, so the process can continue.

When dry yeast is mixed with warm water and sugar, it is "awakened" and begins the fermentation process. As the sugar is converted into gaseous matter, bubbles appear on the surface of the mixture. When this mixture is added to the flour, the yeast begins to work on the sugar contained in the flour and to multiply in the dough.

As you knead the ingredients together, they become thoroughly mixed. Your handling of the dough "develops" the gluten: the complicated particles that make up gluten are aligned into microscopically fine, elastic "threads." It is these gluten threads that give properly kneaded dough its satiny, elastic feel. The longer you knead—up to a certain point—the finer and more elastic the threads become.

When the dough is set in a warm place, the yeast cells really get to work multiplying and producing carbon dioxide. The gas is trapped in the dough, forming bubbles in a network of elastic gluten threads. As the yeast activity continues, increasing quantities of carbon dioxide accumulate; the bubbles of gas increase in size, and the whole mass of dough swells like a great bunch of tiny balloons.

This rising process will continue as long as the network is strong enough to support itself. When the walls of dough surrounding the gas bubbles are stretched too thin, they break; the gas escapes, and the dough collapses. If you poke your finger into risen dough and the dough does not spring back, that indicates that the elastic gluten threads have been stretched to their limit.

Punching the dough down at this point eliminates the carbon dioxide which has formed. It equalizes the temperature throughout the dough. It also enables the gluten threads to realign and regain their elasticity.

The second rising works the same way as the first. It takes less time than the first rising, however, because the dough is warmer and more yeast cells are producing carbon dioxide in it. The second rising allows additional time for enzyme activity to break down the starch, contributing to the flavor and texture of the finished bread. The rising–punching down cycle could theoretically go on until all of the available sugar had been converted, and in fact it can be repeated (if necessary) without hurting the bread; but two risings give the dough good flavor and texture, so we interrupt the cycle at this point by baking the bread.

When the loaf is placed in the oven, it rises suddenly and dramatically during the first few minutes. This "oven spring" has several causes. The sharply rising temperatures speed up the yeast's activity, so a lot of carbon dioxide is produced in a short time. The heat also causes the gases trapped in the dough to expand rapidly. The yeast is gradually inactivated by the heat; when the temperature at the center of the loaf reaches 130 degrees, all the yeast cells are killed. At this stage, the dough is still soft. If you poked the loaf now it would collapse, never to rise again.

At about 130 degrees, the starch granules of the flour begin to swell, absorbing moisture from the other ingredients. As the starch particles swell, they absorb part of the moisture contained in the gluten; the gluten threads become tougher, and the starch granules are embedded in the gluten network. The "gelatinization" of the starch, and the corresponding dehydration of the gluten, continue until the structure of the bread becomes firm.

As the temperature continues to rise, less pressure is exerted by the gases inside the loaf. This reduced pressure coincides with the firming up of the walls that enclosed bubbles of gas, and with the formation of the crust. The alcohol produced by the yeast evaporates from the dough, and moisture escapes in the form of steam. The interior temperature of the loaf never rises above 212 degrees, due to continued evaporation of water and alcohol throughout the baking. But as the surface of the loaf loses moisture, the heat begins to act on the exposed starch and sugar at the surface. When the surface temperature reaches about 230 degrees, the crust begins to change color, as the action of the heat produces yellowish compounds called dextrins. At 320 degrees, the crust becomes brown, as brown dextrins and caramel are produced.

The result of all this botany, chemistry, and physics is a loaf of bread—the same delicious loaf we've been talking about for the past 77 pages. And the processes that turn flour, yeast, and water into bread are the same, whether carried out in your kitchen or in a commercial bakery that turns out seventeen thousand loaves every hour.

Suggestions for Further Baking

NOW THAT YOU HAVE MASTERED THE BASIC TECHNIQUES of bread making, you will probably want to try different kinds of bread recipes in different books. Many bread recipes take longer to make than those in this book, and many kinds of dough are harder to handle; but if you can recognize dough that has been kneaded enough, that has risen enough, that has baked enough, you can probably make any kind of bread you like.

Many all-around cookbooks have recipes for bread, and there are many cookbooks that have only bread recipes. Here are some that I've especially enjoyed.

Beard, James. *Beard on Bread*. New York: Alfred A. Knopf, 1974.

A handsomely designed, clearly written book containing about a hundred recipes for whole meal breads, coffee cakes, rolls, flat breads, batter breads, griddle breads, and more. Each is prefaced with remarks on the bread's history, qualities, and uses.

Brown, Edward Espe. *The Tassajara Bread Book*. Berkeley, California: Shambala Publications, 1970.

The author spent three years as head cook at the Zen monastery at Tassajara. His book, which includes recipes for yeasted bread and pastry, unyeasted bread, sourdough breads, pancakes, muffins, and desserts, has a serene, cheerful personality all its own, favoring whole grains, unrefined sweetenings, and personal involvement.

Dworkin, Floss, and Dworkin, Stan. *Bake Your Own Bread and Be Healthier*. New York: NAL Signet, 1973.

A chatty yet businesslike paperback, with a common-sense approach. The author has taught bread-baking classes and has incorporated her observations into the instructions. The bread baker is encouraged to relax and enjoy it. "Natural ingredients" like sea salt, honey, and unbleached flour are called for in all recipes.

About the Author
and Photographer

HANNAH SOLOMON was born in Los Angeles, California, and has lived in New York City, Chicago, and Hoboken, New Jersey. A graduate of the University of Chicago, she holds B.A. and M.A. degrees in English. Ms. Solomon works as an editor with a major book publishing firm when she isn't baking bread.

EDWARD STEVENSON was born in New York City and grew up in Los Angeles, California. He is a musician and has worked as a harpsichord maker and film editor. His photographs have illustrated several books, including KNITTING FOR BEGINNERS and CROCHET FOR BEGINNERS.